Pebble® Plus
Bilingüe/ Bilingual

Dinosaurios y animales prehistóricos/Dinosaurs and Prehistoric Animals

Estegosaurio/Stegosaurus

por/by Helen Frost

Traducción/Translation: Dr. Martín Luis Guzmán Ferrer

Editor Consultor/Consulting Editor: Dra. Gail Saunders-Smith

Consultor/Consultant: Jack Horner, Curator of Paleontology
Museum of the Rockies
Bozeman, Montana

Capstone
press®

Mankato, Minnesota

Pebble Plus is published by Capstone Press,
151 Good Counsel Drive, P.O. Box 669, Mankato, Minnesota 56002.
www.capstonepress.com

1 2 3 4 5 6 11 10 09 08 07 06

Library of Congress Cataloging-in-Publication Data
Frost, Helen, 1949–
    [Stegosaurus. Spanish & English]
    Estegosaurio = Stegosaurus/de/by Helen Frost.
    p. cm. —(Pebble Plus. Dinosaurios y animales prehistóricos = Pebble Plus. Dinosaurs and
prehistoric animals)
    Includes index.
    ISBN-13: 978-0-7368-6684-2 (hardcover)
    ISBN-10: 0-7368-6684-1 (hardcover)
    ISBN-13: 978-1-4296-1184-8 (softcover pbk.)
    ISBN-10: 1-4296-1184-7 (softcover pbk.)
    1. Stegosaurus—Juvenile literature. I. Title: Stegosaurus. II. Title. III. Pebble Plus. Dinosaurios y
animales prehistóricos.
QE862.O65F77718 2007
567.915'3—dc22   2005037475

Summary: Simple text and illustrations present stegosaurus, its body parts, and behavior—in both English
    and Spanish.

Interactive ISBN-13: 978-0-7368-7908-8
Interactive ISBN-10: 0-7368-7908-0

Editorial Credits
Martha E. H. Rustad, editor; Katy Kudela, bilingual editor; Eida del Risco, Spanish copy editor; Linda Clavel,
    set designer; Jon Hughes, illustrator; Wanda Winch, photo researcher; Scott Thoms, photo editor

Photo Credit
David Liebman, 20–21

The author thanks the children's library staff at the Allen County Public Library in Fort Wayne, Indiana,
for research assistance.

Note to Parents and Teachers

The Dinosaurios y animales prehistóricos/Dinosaurs and Prehistoric Animals set
supports national science standards related to the evolution of life. This book describes
stegosaurus in both English and Spanish. The images support early readers in
understanding the text. The repetition of words and phrases helps early readers learn
new words. This book also introduces early readers to subject-specific vocabulary words,
which are defined in the Glossary section. Early readers may need assistance to read
some words and to use the Table of Contents, Glossary, Internet Sites, and Index sections
of the book.

Table of Contents

Tabla de contenidos

A Dinosaur with Plates

Stegosaurus was a dinosaur
with bony plates on its back.
The plates were shaped
like triangles.

Un dinosaurio con placas

El estegosaurio era un dinosaurio
con placas huesudas en la espalda.
Las placas tenían forma de triángulo.

Stegosaurus lived
in prehistoric times.
It lived about 150 million
years ago in forests
and swamps.

El estegosaurio vivió en tiempos
prehistóricos. Vivió hace cerca
de 150 millones de años en
los bosques y pantanos.

How Stegosaurus Looked

Stegosaurus was almost
as long as a school bus.
It was about 25 feet
(8 meters) long.

Cómo eran los estegosaurios

El estegosaurio era tan largo como
un autobús escolar. Medía cerca
de 8 metros (25 pies) de largo.

8

Stegosaurus had
a thick body
and a small head.

El estegosaurio tenía
el cuerpo grueso y
la cabeza pequeña.

Stegosaurus had
two short front legs.
It had two long back legs.

El estegosaurio tenía cortas
las dos patas delanteras.
Sus dos patas traseras
eran largas.

Stegosaurus had sharp spikes on its tail. It used the spikes to protect itself.

El estegosaurio tenía unas púas afiladas en la cola. Usaba estas púas para defenderse.

What Stegosaurus Did

Stegosaurus walked slowly.

It drank water from streams.

Qué hacían los estegosaurios

El estegosaurio caminaba despacio.

Bebía agua de los ríos.

Stegosaurus ate leaves
and plants. Its mouth
was shaped like a beak.

El estegosaurio comía hojas
y plantas. Su boca tenía
forma de pico.

The End of Stegosaurus

Stegosaurus died out

about 145 million years ago.

No one knows why they all died.

You can see stegosaurus fossils

in museums.

El fin del estegosaurio

El estegosaurio desapareció hace cerca

de 145 millones de años. Nadie sabe

por qué todos murieron. Se pueden ver

fósiles de estegosaurios en los museos.

A Solar-Powered Dinosaur?

Glossary

beak—the hard, pointed part of an animal's mouth

dinosaur—a large reptile that lived on land in prehistoric times

forest—a large area covered with trees and plants

fossil—the remains or traces of an animal or a plant, preserved as rock

museum—a place where interesting objects of art, history, or science are shown

plate—a flat, bony growth

prehistoric—very, very old; prehistoric means belonging to a time before history was written down.

spike—a hard, pointy object; the spikes on the tail of stegosaurus were made of bone.

swamp—an area of wet, spongy ground

Glosario

el bosque—gran superficie cubierta de árboles y plantas

el dinosaurio—reptil grande de la prehistoria que vivía en tierra

el fósil—restos o vestigios de un animal o una planta que se conservan como piedras

el museo—lugar donde se exhiben objetos de arte, historia o ciencias

el pantano—superficie de tierra anegada en agua

el pico—parte dura y puntiaguda de la boca de un animal

la placa—protuberancia plana y huesuda

prehistórico—muy, muy viejo; prehistórico quiere decir perteneciente a una época antes de que hubiera historia escrita.

la púa—objeto duro y puntiagudo; las púas en la cola del estegosaurio eran de hueso.

Internet Sites

FactHound offers a safe, fun way to find Internet sites related to this book. All of the sites on FactHound have been researched by our staff.

Here's how:

1. Visit *www.facthound.com*

2. Choose your grade level.

3. Type in this book ID **0736866841** for age-appropriate sites. You may also browse subjects by clicking on letters, or by clicking on pictures and words.

4. Click on the **Fetch It** button.

FactHound will fetch the best sites for you!

Sitios de Internet

FactHound proporciona una manera divertida y segura de encontrar sitios de Internet relacionados con este libro. Nuestro personal ha investigado todos los sitios de FactHound. Es posible que los sitios no estén en español.

Se hace así:

1. Visita *www.facthound.com*

2. Elige tu grado escolar.

3. Introduce este código especial **0736866841** para ver sitios apropiados según tu edad, o usa una palabra relacionada con este libro para hacer una búsqueda general.

4. Haz clic en el botón **Fetch It**.

¡FactHound buscará los mejores sitios para ti!

Index

Índice